WHAT DO I DO NOW?

**A resource bank of English Language
extension activities for the primary school**

Josephine Steel
Lynn Taylor

TES
SCOTLAND

Hodder Gibson

A MEMBER OF THE HODDER HEADLINE GROUP

Acknowledgements

We would like to thank the staff of St Nicholas' Primary in Broxburn, Alexander Peden Primary in Harthill, St Mary's Primary in Bathgate, St Thomas' Primary in Wishaw and Cathedral Primary in Motherwell for their help with the research for this book.

I would like to take this opportunity to thank all of my family and friends for all of their support and encouragement. A big thank you to Alan for believing in me, and my three wee angels Nicola, Matthew and Niamh for their cuddles.

Josephine Steel

Thanks to my family for their support throughout this project, especially Stewart – thank you for the supply of chocolate and love. And a huge thanks to the crowd of ladies on madmums.com   *Lynn Taylor*

The Publishers would like to thank the following for permission to reproduce copyright material:

Photo credits
All photos by Lynn Taylor

Acknowledgements
Every effort has been made to trace all copyright holders, but if any have been inadvertently overlooked the Publishers will be pleased to make the necessary arrangements at the first opportunity.

Although every effort has been made to ensure that website addresses are correct at time of going to press, Hodder Gibson cannot be held responsible for the content of any website mentioned in this book. It is sometimes possible to find a relocated web page by typing in the address of the home page for a website in the URL window of your browser.

Hodder Headline's policy is to use papers that are natural, renewable and recyclable products and made from wood grown in sustainable forests. The logging and manufacturing processes are expected to conform to the environmental regulations of the country of origin.

Orders: please contact Bookpoint Ltd, 130 Milton Park, Abingdon, Oxon OX14 4SB. Telephone: (44) 01235 827720. Fax: (44) 01235 400454. Lines are open 9.00 – 5.00, Monday to Saturday, with a 24-hour message answering service. Visit our website at www.hoddereducation.co.uk. Hodder Gibson can be contacted direct on: Tel: 0141 848 1609; Fax: 0141 889 6315; email: hoddergibson@hodder.co.uk

© Josephine Steel and Lynn Taylor 2006
First published in 2006 by
Hodder Gibson, an imprint of Hodder Education,
a member of the Hodder Headline Group,
2a Christie Street
Paisley PA1 1NB

Impression number   5 4 3 2 1
Year   2010 2009 2008 2007 2006

Cover illustration by Lynn Taylor
Illustrations by Lynn Taylor
Typeset in Formata Light 9/12pt by DCGraphic Design Limited, Swanley Village, Kent.
Printed in Scotland by CPI Bath

A catalogue record for this title is available from the British Library

ISBN-10: 0-340-91367-3
ISBN-13: 978-0-340-91367-3

Contents

Foreword

The *Times Educational Supplement Scotland* is delighted to be associated with the publication of this series of books aimed at Scottish primary teachers, and devoted to the practical classroom realities of continuing professional development.

Since the newspaper's birth in 1965, we have always attempted to inform, educate, and occasionally entertain the Scottish teaching profession, as well as to encourage dialogue between all educational sectors. In recent years, our commitment to the concept of encouraging educationists to constantly reflect – and act – upon best practice has been most tangibly evident in the provision of an annual CPD supplement. This offers full and detailed examination of developments in CPD from both Scottish and international contexts, and attempts to share best practice in a manner that is both accessible and pedagogically sound.

Each week, we provide a wide range of educational news items, supplemented by practical teaching strategies, as well as a host of free ideas on our website www.tes.co.uk/resources/. But this series of books offers specifically Scottish resources written by practising Scottish primary teachers. They provide an exciting range of completely practical strategies, techniques, inspirational ideas – and many photocopiable resources – with which to develop teachers' professionalism in the day-to-day realities of Scotland's primary classrooms.

We very much hope that they succeed in enhancing satisfaction and motivation for teachers, as well as making a valuable contribution to their continuing professional development.

Neil Munro
Editor, *Times Educational Supplement Scotland*

Chapter One

Why should I bother with extension activities?

Is this scenario familiar to you?

> 'I'm finished… What do I do now?'
>
> 'It can't be possible,' you think. 'That should take at least 20 minutes to complete!'
>
> The voice has turned into a child who is now patting you on the arm while they repeat their cry of 'What do I do now?'

Now let's be honest. What would your usual reply be? Take a jigsaw? A scrap piece of paper maybe? Go read a book? Not a very inspiring return for working so well.

So what shall we do? Instead of trying to just 'fill up' this time we know that we should try to use it as an opportunity to extend and reinforce learning. Obviously, we also have the added pressure that children should be undertaking Language activities in their designated Language time to meet the demands of the structure and balance of the curriculum. But…

Oh no! I hear you cry. Will this mean more planning? More teaching? More marking? Please, please no more. It's hard enough to get through the already growing workload.

If only there were activities that required little planning, no extra teaching, no extra marking, no extra photocopying, were completely re-usable and allowed the children to take ownership of how they can extend their own learning when they have finished their work (and is linked to our Scottish 5–14 Curriculum into the bargain). Does this sound any better? Well that's the aim of this book!

What Do I Do Now? provides extension activities in English Language in particular, because children are always reading, writing, talking and listening no matter which subject they are learning in. Let's face it: the children need to have these core skills in order to access the whole curriculum fully. The activities featured are focused on building these skills in an enjoyable and independent way. In fact, half the time they won't even know they're learning!

Resourcing extension activities

You probably have more resources to hand than you think.

The first thing to do is have a good stock-take of the resources in your class or that you have at your disposal. How many games or activities lie unused or little used? Why? Do the children not know how to use them? Do you not trust them to keep them in good shape? Are they doing any good, either to you or the children, sitting in their packaging?

Well, I'm sure we are all agreed that the best thing to do is get all of our resources out to be used in the class. Take the time to explain their proper use. This will save you much, much more time and energy in the future. Ensure that part of this 'training' is the retrieval and restoration of the resources so that they can be independently accessed. This may sound fairly obvious, but how often do you have to leave what you are doing to retrieve a game or activity for the children to do?

The next thing to do is distinguish which area of the curriculum each of these resources falls under. The last thing you want to do is fill your Language time with Maths games and activities.

But what if you don't have many resources or, after auditing, you find that there is an imbalance in curricular resources. What then? Do you go to your head teacher begging for money to redress the balance? It is often hard enough to find the money for the necessities of the curriculum, never mind all the extras. Well, you have made the first step in redressing that imbalance by buying this book! We have compiled a number of tried and tested resources and projects suitable for every stage of the primary school. And they are linked to the Scottish 5–14 Curriculum. (Hooray – were you fed up with all those books based on Key Stages too – being a Scottish teacher is like converting the pound to the euro!)

Figure 01.01 **"It's like converting the Pound to the Euro"**

Chapter Two

Organising for extension activities

Creating an interactive classroom

Before we begin, let's stop.

We would just like to reassure you that …

> **… Our approach to extension activities requires no extra marking and most are completely re-useable.**

Ah, now we've got that off our chest, let's begin again.

We have written this book because we felt there was a real need for appropriate valuable extension activities in our own classrooms. Through our research we found that we were not alone…

We can now, finally, admit our guilty secret. When faced with the question that echoes round every school in the land – 'What do I do now?' we would often reply 'Erm, go and get a library book/scrap paper / look under your desk for five things to pick up / go and have a wee rest by putting your head on the table for a minute…'

Meanwhile we are constantly replenishing our scrap paper trays as fast as the children are emptying them. This results in paper mountains in school bags, or as endless tokens of affection to us. How many scrap sheets of paper do we possess at the end of a typical school day which we promise will go onto our fridges at home – but we all know where those go, don't we?

So instead of providing fodder for the bin we decided that the children should actually be doing useful, engaging tasks appropriate to the subject they are covering at the time; something they can actually learn from and expand their knowledge and skills with. A novel idea, eh?

Yes, yes, we know you agree. But as teachers ourselves we know how hard it is to plan our day-to-day core lessons and activities, never mind plan endless tasks for those fabulous fast finishers. Endless photocopying of worksheets adds to this dilemma. Not only did our head teachers hate our massive photocopy bills but also the corrections spiralled out of control, not to mention the problem of where to file this endless stream of paper… So we decided to take the bull by the horns and try to address this.

When we first looked at the provision of extension activities, we wanted to cover all areas of the curriculum in one fell swoop. It soon became evident that the resources we had for Language alone would fill up a book. And so *What Do I Do Now?* was born.

At this point we have to be honest. The set-up of these extension activities will take some organisation on the part of the teacher. But what worthwhile teaching aid doesn't?

What we do promise is that the effort put in to get the activities and projects up and running will be saved time and time again by the cessation of the endless explanation of worksheets and answering the dreaded question, 'What do I do now?'

Most of the activities and projects come in the form of a workcard or sheet. These are intended to be copied and laminated to extend their working life and, of course, to make them re-usable.

Laminating pouches and dry-wipe pens are not *the* cheapest to buy, but weighing that up against 25 to 30 copies of *everything,* it seems not too bad. Making them dry-wipe also gives freedom to the children to get it wrong, try something different or change their answer easily. Of course, this is not to say that you couldn't use these resources as photocopiable activities, but ask yourself: how many times have children in your class completed a learning task and you wish that they could do it all over again? By making these resources re-usable, the children can revisit the activity as many times as they like – each time bringing more knowledge with them.

The tasks work very well as paired or trio activities. They are a great stimulus for talking and listening (oh yes – another box ticked!). The format of each is simple and does not require laborious explanations, freeing up your time to work with group or individuals who require your attention

Again we would like to stress that these activities are **not meant to be corrected**. It is very liberating for a child to do some work that is not going to be marked all over with the teacher's pen. They are doing it for themselves and can have their own agenda. Of course it is very liberating for us too – all we need to do is lose the guilt. *You don't have to correct something to make it valid.* Ask yourself: do you correct those scrap pieces of paper or completed jigsaws?

Something we are sure you will notice is that there seem to be more photocopiable resources for the infants in this book. Well – wait for it – there is a reason for that. As we all know, the older and more responsible children get, the less we need to spoon-feed them with constant extension activities and structure. Their normal class lessons and activities take longer and their ability to stay on-task grows. But don't worry; there is certainly lots in here for older pupils too. It is just that not as much of it is of the photocopiable variety. There are lots of ideas and projects, which will keep children working.

Organising the resources

As previously mentioned, it's important to know what resources you have in your class. One teacher we met didn't realise she had a whole array of coloured plasticine because she hadn't looked in a box at the bottom of her cupboard! These resources need to be organised. This is where the time needs to be spent in bringing out all of your resources: evaluating if they're of any use to you, and sorting them into curricular areas.

We have discovered a brilliant, simple way to organise extension resources for easy use by the children.

When you have organised your resources into curricular areas, colour code them, for example green for Language, red for Maths, and so on. Then you can make a selection of the activities you want the children to choose from that week. (It's a good idea to offer a limited choice of resources and rotate them on a weekly basis rather than having all of everything out all the time. You can then choose activities that are appropriate to the children's age, stage and interests.)

Organising extension resources in this way makes the task of labelling so much easier to do. Instead of trying to make what seem like a thousand different labels to cover all of the resources you have, you simply need to have a coloured label to represent each of the different curricular activities. The children will then know by looking at their task board that they have to choose from the 'green' activities when they have completed their Language learning task.

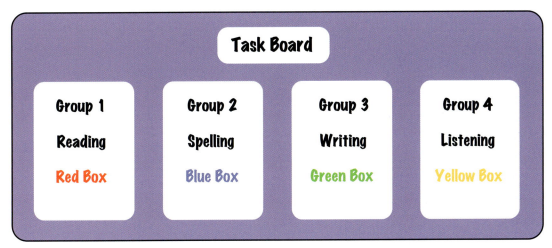

Task Board

Group 1	Group 2	Group 3	Group 4
Reading	Spelling	Writing	Listening
Red Box	Blue Box	Green Box	Yellow Box

Figure 01.02 A simplified task board showing follow up "boxed" activities. Each of the colour coded boxes contains a follow up language activity suitable to the ability of the children

The class library

There is an emphasis on the importance of the class library in all of the Primary Practicals books in this series. By making room for a class library, and looking after it, you are showing the children how important and worthwhile books are.

If you are lucky you will already have a library with bright labels, interesting books and a cosy seating area. If not, then trust us, you have the ability to make it that way. By taking time and care over the creation of your class library you are sending the children a positive message about the importance of literature. Many learning opportunities can be made for the children from the class library.

Choose a place in the classroom that is slightly separated from the hustle and bustle (not easy, we know), – a corner, for example. Make the library welcoming: a happy, cosy place to be. For example, drape a piece of material from the ceiling over the library to soften the look and make it 'homely' by adding old clean cushions and pillows and even some soft toys for infant classes. A plant or fish will add some life to the area.

Display the books so that the children will be encouraged to choose. Make a simple 'book of the week' sign (we have provided a template for this in the photocopiable resources section of *The Complete Classroom Organiser*), and highlight either a book or author for the children to discover, or thematic books linked to class topics.

If you don't have a large area to devote to your library, then don't panic. Use a couple of cardboard boxes covered in attractive paper to display your books.

Photograph 01.02 **A small class library**

Never leave books that are ripped or past their best on display. Would you choose a book from your local library that was damaged? Neither will the children! It's better to change the entire selection of books in the library every few weeks, perhaps at the start of each planning block. Instead of having your full quota of library books out on display, hold some back in order to keep the children's interest in the books.

Use labels for 'Fiction' and 'Non-Fiction' to teach the differentiation between the two. This can be taught from Primary 1.

Children can have ownership of their class library by taking it in turns to be the class librarian who will be responsible for tidying and arranging the books back to their 'Fiction' and 'Non-fiction' homes. Older children can also be responsible for recording the books chosen by their classmates.

Alphabetical order can be taught in a real sense through encouraging the children to organise the library shelves. You can even make this simpler by setting aside a selection of a few books in a box for individuals or pairs to organise.

Placing a bit of thought into your library space makes it interesting for the children – and you won't feel so guilty about asking the children to 'go and choose a book'!

Talking and listening

Many teachers groan silently when it comes to the inclusion of talking and listening in our English Language curriculum. We believe that it shouldn't be treated entirely as a stand-alone subject. Talking and listening rely heavily on each other and are integral to all that we do in school. The most natural and meaningful way to cover talking and listening is to give the children as much opportunity as we can to participate in activities that require them to talk and listen to their peers and adults. If we are honest, contrived listening activities are little more than a time filler in most classes. Effective communication is such an important life skill and it should be fostered in class. Extension activities can be an effective way of ensuring you are providing opportunities for talking and listening.

In infant classes you can encourage the development of talking and listening through structured play activities. Structured play needn't involve grandiose resources on a large scale – you can encourage talking and listening through having, for example:

✔ some plastic cups, spoons and plates for an imaginary tea party

✔ small models of farm animals

✔ role play

✔ dolls and (clean) soft toys

✔ puppets

✔ empty food cartons and a till to make a tabletop shop

✔ a tray of sand with small hidden items – this makes an exciting treasure hunt

✔ a few old big cardboard boxes – see what the children can do with these.

In all stages of the primary school you can always encourage talking and listening by setting a pair of children on a task, as opposed to always looking for individual responses.

A listening centre is often a little used resource. For most of us it just seems too much hassle. Finding taped stories with matching books is bad enough and then there is the problem of working the machine! Sometimes it seems much easier to leave well alone. But let's think about it. Most children will be used to using far more sophisticated audio equipment at home or will already be familiar with listening centres from their nursery establishment, so learning the purpose of a few buttons should really be no problem. A green sticker on the play and a red one on the stop button helps simplify matters, too.

When it comes to finding listening resources, why not record, some stories yourself? If you are looking at a specific author or book of the week, it doesn't take long to record it onto tape to let the children listen to it in small groups. Why not record the reading books for each group? Keep a separate tape for each, then record one story after another and before you know it you'll have a whole bank of stories. It is important that the children listen to model readers on a regular basis so that they get used to hearing expression, intonation and fluency. Don't be embarrassed about them listening to your voice – they listen to it every day anyway, and who would be more natural to listen to than you?

Try giving the children access to the recording equipment. Allow them to record themselves reading once they have finished their work, and then to listen back to their own voice. Yes, there will be a few giggles when they do this at first, but after a few times they get used to it and enjoy hearing themselves read. It is really useful for them to know how they sound when they read and they can evaluate themselves at the same time.

Instead of always using taped stories, try recording some information/non-fiction books instead. To extend this the children could practise taking down one or two notes to fill out a 'Fantastic Facts' sheet.

Another idea to extend the children's listening opportunities is to record a set of drawing instructions onto tape that the children can follow. They can be as simple or as complicated as you like: simple shapes to be coloured in or scenes with suns, clouds, trees, etc. Seasonal drawing instructions are also fun – 'Are you imagining a snowman with three buttons, two sticks for arms…?' Just make sure you don't talk too quickly, and give them time to complete each stage.

If technology allows, you could always burn all of this onto a CD and, hey presto, no rewinding or fast forwarding.

Writing boxes

Writing boxes provide children with a treasure trove of writing ideas and materials. It is a good idea to timetable this activity.

First of all get a sturdy box with a lid large enough to accommodate A4 paper (a well-known Swedish company does these very cheaply). Then fill it up with lots of lovely stationery items:

✔ pens
✔ coloured pencils
✔ gel/glitter pens
✔ sticky tape
✔ glue sticks
✔ stapler
✔ coloured dry-wipe markers
✔ coloured stampers
✔ scissors

etc…

The activities within the box have to be stimulating and inviting. Below are some ideas – but the list is not exhaustive. Some of the activities in our photocopiable section are suitable for use in a writing box. We're sure that the children in your class will come up with some of their own ideas, too.

✔ Laminated celebration cards
✔ Note paper, thank-you cards and invitations
✔ Menus
✔ Postcards
✔ Shaped writing paper
✔ Alphabet dot to dots
✔ A selection of forms
✔ Recipe cards
✔ Sticky notelets (to be displayed on a class notice board)
✔ A selection of certificates and awards to give to their peers

Don't put everything in the box at the same time. Keep to three or four activities at any one time and change and rotate them on a regular basis. If most of the resources are laminated they should last all year.

This resource provides the opportunity for children to write at their own pace.

If you have the luxury of having lots of space in your classroom you could have a writing table where all of the resources could be kept.

Upper school projects

We end this section with a look at some of the upper school independent learning projects you can provide in your class.

- **Lucky dip story bag.** Place different objects (for example an old key, a necklace, ornament and so on) in a bag for the children to select from in order to stimulate a short story, poem, cartoon, etc.

- **Mark the text.** Photocopy a few pages of texts that the children are interested in and encourage them to use highlighters to mark the text at points where they like the author's use of description or language features, for example. This activity works well in pairs and trios. The children could also keep a **'Good ideas'** book in which they can note down any aspects of a writer's craft they appreciate, for use in their own work.

- **Class novels.** We have provided suggested titles for class novels in our photocopiable resources section. The only limit to where the class novel goes lies with the extent of the children's imaginations! You can have several of these on the go at the same time to allow all of the children in the class to contribute. Some children may also like to have their own novel on the go.

- **Class magazine or radio programme.** This is always a winner. The production of a class magazine or pre-recorded radio show requires the children to develop their skills in all aspects of the English Language curriculum. The children could be assigned different editorial jobs to do in order to produce the magazine or programme. They could have reporter notebooks to hand in order to note down any school news or ideas they may have. Encourage the children to explore emotive subjects from both sides through assignments relating to the magazine or show's production.

Chapter Three
Photocopiable Resources

The following photocopiable sheets have been provided for your use. For each of the extension activities in the list below, an introduction linking it to the Scottish 5-14 Curriculum is included.

Pointy Poles

Sequencing Jigsaws

Story Cubes

Handwriting Alphabet Cards

Sound Snake

Alphabet Fun

Word Octopus

Letters and Postcards

Blank Greetings Cards

Story Starts

Where Am I?

Rewrite the Sentence

True/False/Can't tell!

Fix the Story

Make It Better

Alphabetical Order Ideas

Who, What, Where, Why?

Story Wordbanks

Sentence Bumpers

How Many Words?

Form Fillers

Recipe Card

Café Menu

Newspaper Report

Find the Vowel

Dictionary Bookmarks

Novel Titles

Anything but Said!

Boring to Brilliant

Punctuate!

Award

Play Dough Recipes

5-14 Mapping Grid

	Point Poles	Sequencing Jigsaws	Story Cubes	Handwriting Alphabet	Sound Snake	Alphabet Fun	Word Octopus	Letters and Postcards	Blank Greeting Cards	Story Starts	Where am I?	Re-write the Sentence	True, False, Can't tell	Fix the Story	Make it Better	Alphabetical Order Ideas	Who, What, Where, Why?	Story Wordbanks	Sentence Bumpers	How Many Words?	Form Fillers	Recipe Card	Café Menu	Newspaper Report	Find the Vowel	Dictionary Bookmarks	Novel Titles	Anything But Said!	Boring to Brilliant	Punctuate!	Award
Reading																															
Reading for enjoyment	A																A B														
Reading for information	A	A B												A																	
Knowledge about language															A	ALL	ALL										B C D	C D	C D	C D	
Awareness of genre		A B															A B													C D	
Spelling					A																										
Writing																															
Functional writing		A B						A B	A B	A B											A B	A B	A B	C D E							ALL
Imaginative writing			ALL						A B						A			A B									C D E				
Personal writing									A B																						
Knowledge about language									A B			A B		A	ALL		A B	A B	ALL	ALL				C D E	B C		C D E			C D	
Punctuation and structure									A B	A B	A B	A B		A	ALL		A B		ALL					C D E	B C		C D E	C D		C D	
Handwriting and presentation			A	A				A B	A B															C D E							
Spelling			A	A		A		A B		A B					ALL			A B	ALL	ALL				C D E			C D E				
Talking																															
Conveying information, instructions and directions		A B									A B																				
Talking in groups			ALL								A B								ALL												
Audience awareness			ALL								A B																				
Listening																															
Listening for information, instructions and directions		A B									A B																				
Listening in groups			ALL								A B								ALL												

Pointy Poles

5–14 Link – Level A

Reading: Reading for information
Reading for enjoyment

Oh how the children will love these! They are so simple, but very effective. These are simply small sticks (a ruler will do) or folded-over thick card with a pointy finger arrow on the end. The children use these to point to and read all the words displayed in the classroom. These words don't just need to be in word lists but could be on displays, labelled trays and materials. Most infant classes are 'text drenched' with everything labelled from desk to plant to book corner to sink! These poles actively encourage the children to read and take notice of environmental print. They are a licence to wander around the class with a purpose! If the children get stuck with a word they can copy it down. They can then ask you later, or ask a friend to help them with their 'hard' words. Believe us – this one is a winner.

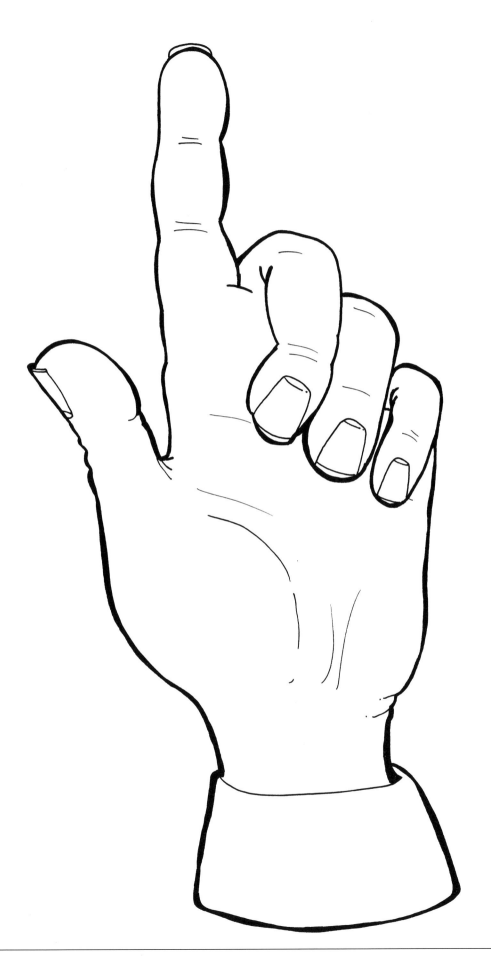

Sequencing Jigsaws

5–14 Link – Levels A and B

Reading: **Reading for information**
Awareness of genre

Writing: **Functional writing**

Talking: **Conveying information, instructions and directions**

Listening: **Listening for information, instructions and directions**

These can be used as jigsaws or as a stimulus for functional writing or talking and listening, depending on the stage and ability of the children.

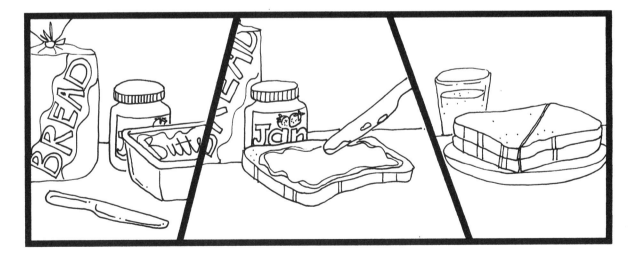

Sequencing jigsaws

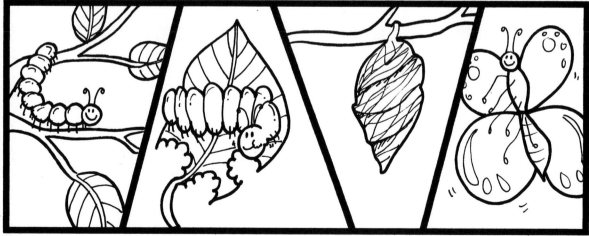

Sequencing jigsaws

Story Cubes

5–14 Link – All levels

Talking: **Talking in groups**
Audience awareness

Writing: **Imaginative writing**

Listening: Listening in groups

There are six different ready-made story cubes included in this book, and one blank one. The story cubes act as a stimulus to enable children to create their own stories either verbally or in written form. They establish for the children **who** is in their story, **where** their story is happening and **what action** is happening. The stories can be sensible but you can also encourage the children to let their imaginations run riot with the suggestions from the cubes. They are the authors, it's their story!

The children can individually, in pairs or small groups throw all three to make a random selection of each. Tell the children that it is the top-facing picture that has to be used.

Photocopy the story cubes onto thin card and laminate them before cutting them out.

Teacher Tip

Lay a ruler along each edge of the laminated cube net and draw a blunt knife along the line to give a sharper fold.

Who? story cube

Who? story cube

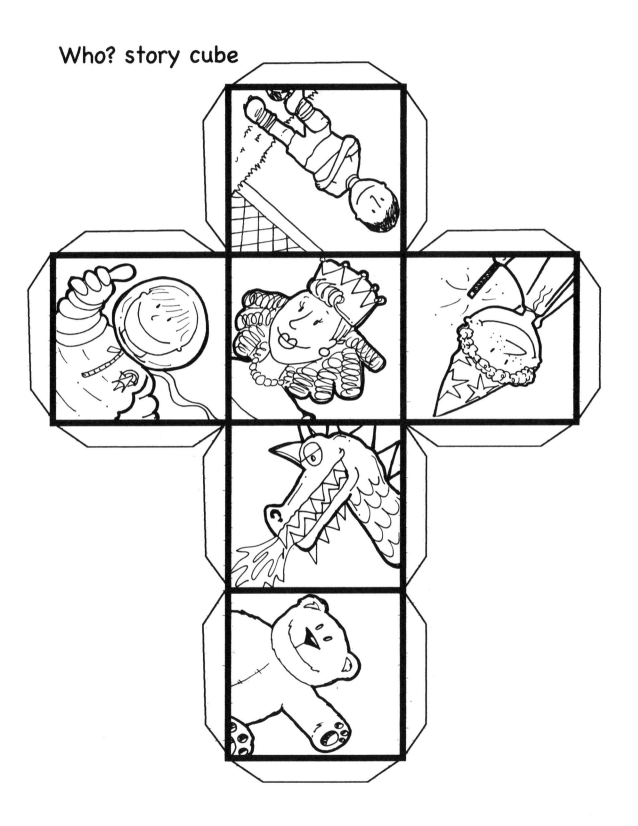

Where? story cube

Where? story cube

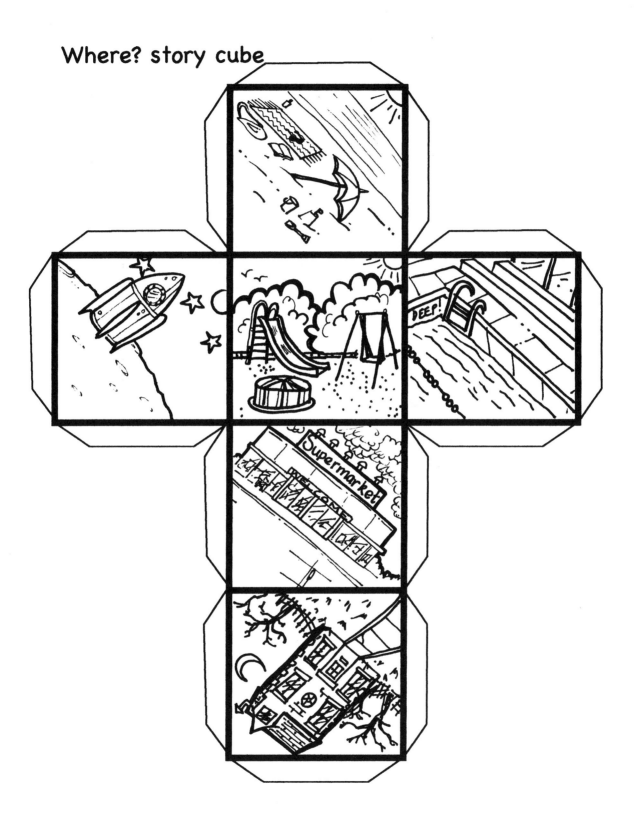

What? story cube

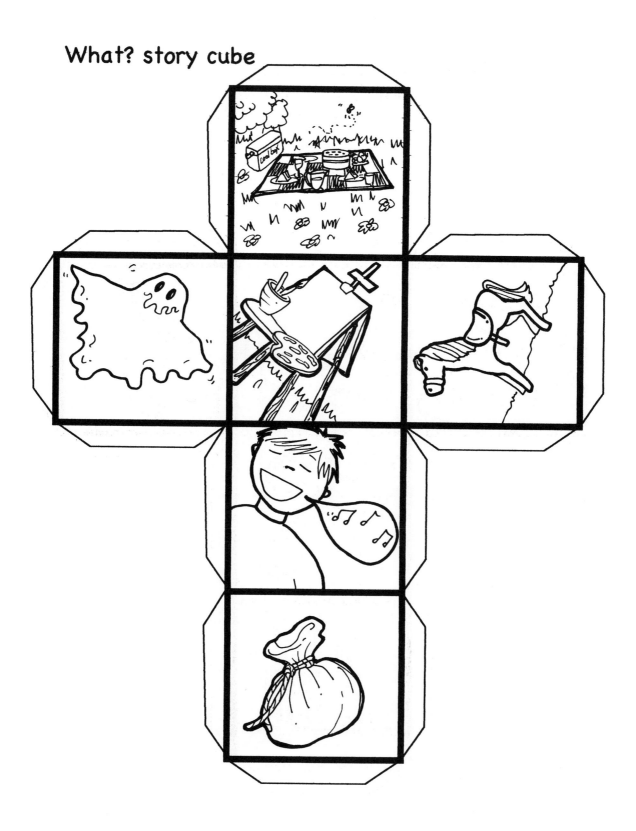

What? story cube

Blank story cube

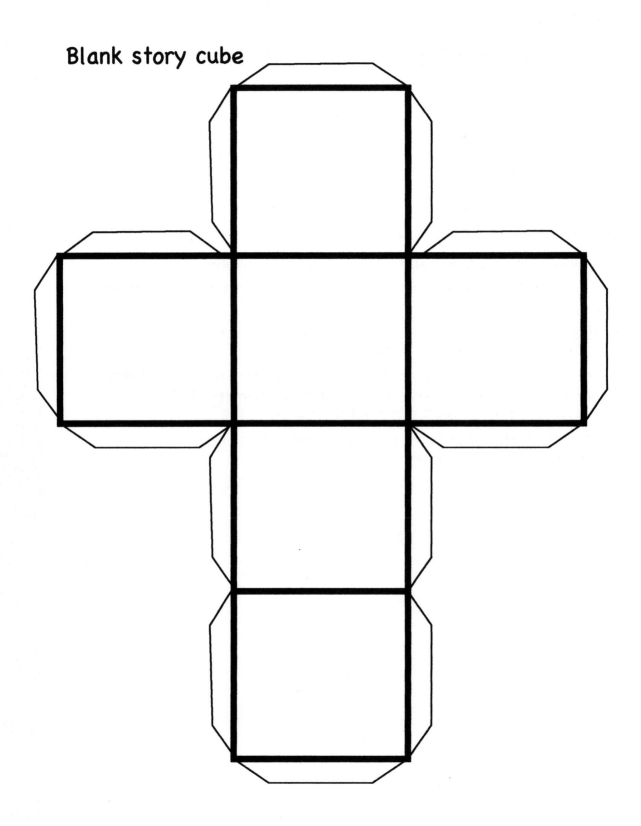

Handwriting Alphabet Cards

5–14 Link – Level A

Writing: Handwriting and presentation
Spelling

We have provided a set of alphabet cards featuring both upper and lower case letters and a picture clue to the sound. They have dots and arrows indicating where the formation of each letter begins. The font we have used to create the cards is called 'Chalkboard': we have chosen that style in particular because it is easy to change to suit most school's needs, for example to add 'flicks' to the end of the letters. There are also four patterned cards that will help develop the children's fine motor skills for handwriting.

The cards can be used in a number of ways.

✔ They can be coloured, laminated and used to order the alphabet.

✔ Once laminated they can be used by the children to practise their letter formation by using dry-wipe pens.

✔ The pictures can be covered over before they are copied and the copied cards cut in half – then the children can match upper to lower case.

✔ They can be enlarged on the photocopier and placed into plastic display pockets and then the children can make the letters by using play dough. (We have included a couple of recipes for dough at the end of this book.)

✔ They can be enlarged for use on class wall displays or hung from a washing line with pegs at the children's level.

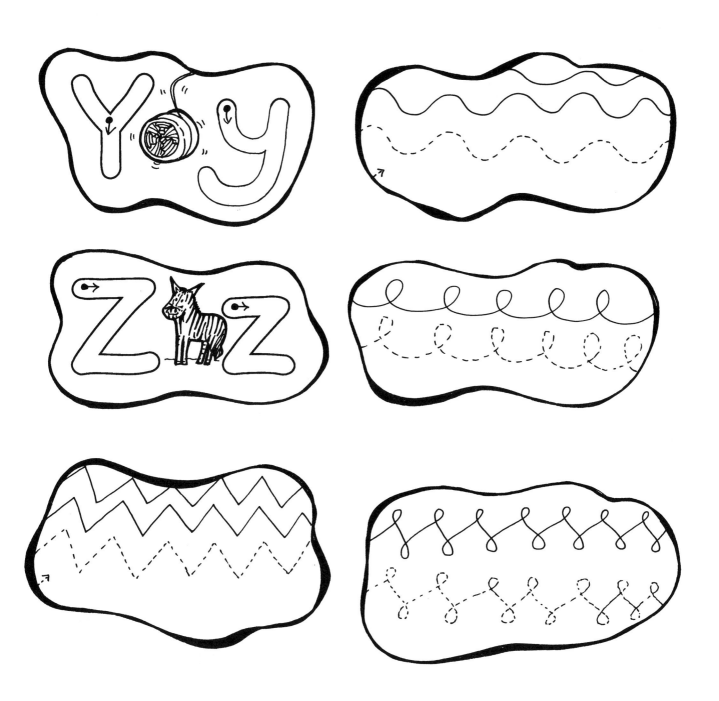

Sound Snake

5–14 Link – Level A

Writing: Handwriting and presentation
Spelling

This activity speaks for itself. The sounds (letters) can be changed before copying to suit your needs.

Sound Snake

Fill in the missing letters in the snake below.

Alphabet Fun

5–14 Link – Level A

Reading: Spelling

This resource is aimed at children who are learning or reinforcing their initial sounds and is self-explanatory. Although these sheets are meant to be laminated for repeated use, they can work well as a worksheet too.

Alphabet Fun

Match the lower case letters to the capital letters.

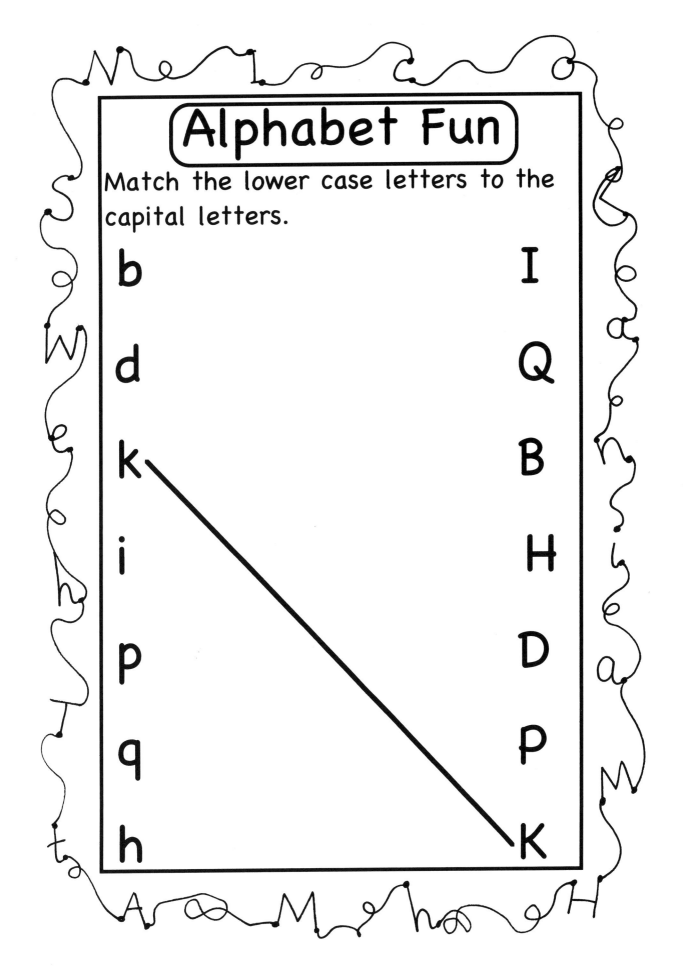

b	I
d	Q
k	B
i	H
p	D
q	P
h	K

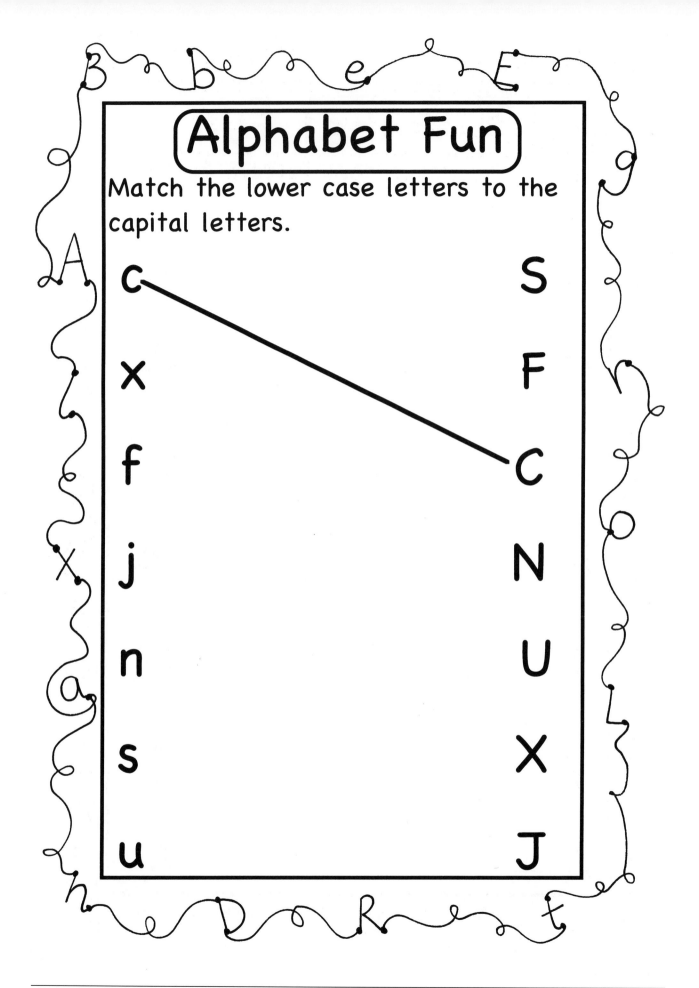

Alphabet Fun

Match the lower case letters to the capital letters.

c   S

x   F

f   C

j   N

n   U

s   X

u   J

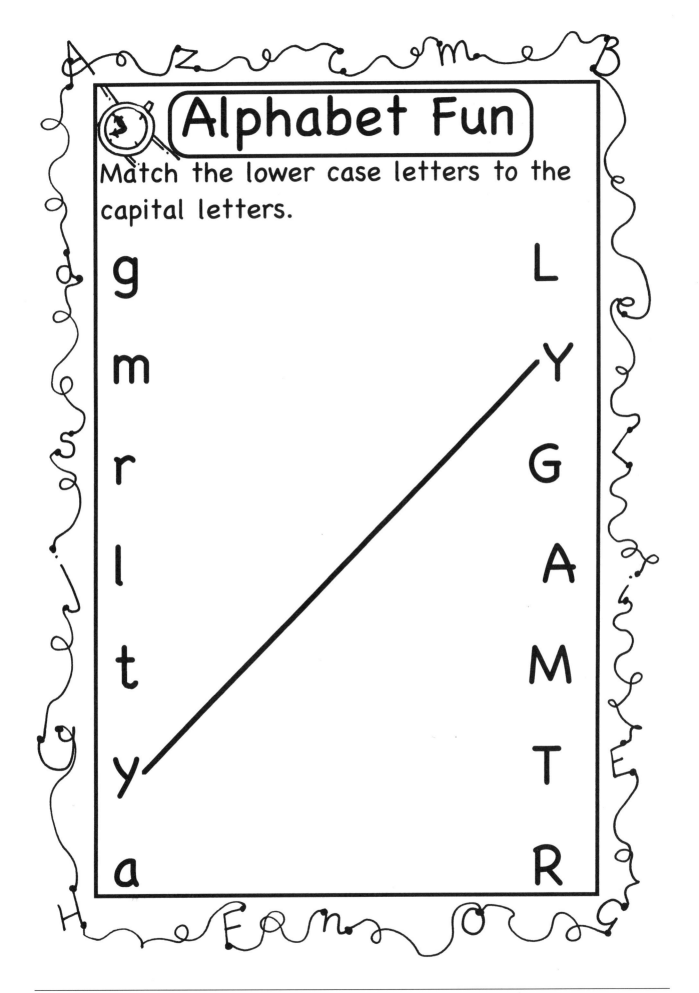

Alphabet Fun

Match the lower case letters to the capital letters.

g

m

r

l

t

y

a

L

Y

G

A

M

T

R

Word Octopus

5–14 Link – Level A

Writing: Spelling

Photocopy and laminate enough boards for a small group to have one each. Write in the centre a stimulus word or a spelling phoneme and challenge the children to fill the rest of the spaces with words relating to the phoneme or word. Set a time to add to the challenge.

Letters and Postcards

5–14 Link – Levels A and B

Writing: **Functional writing**
Personal writing
Punctuation and structure
Spelling
Handwriting and presentation

These provide a good outline for the children to experiment with their letter writing. They are a good resource for the writing box. Three letters are included: Santa letter, thank you letter and a blank template, which can be used for any topic, as well as blank postcards. Why not use some real cards too, of different topics. Laminate them to lengthen their life and rotate them regularly.

Dear Santa,

_____

_____

_____

_____

_____

from

_____

Dear _____,

Thank you _____

_____

_____

_____

_____

_____

_____

_____

Blank Greetings Cards

5–14 Link – Levels A and B

Writing: Functional writing
Punctuation and structure

These are self-explanatory and can be put into the writing box so that the children can always find them. There are some popular topic cards included too – Christmas, Chinese New Year, Eid, Diwali.

Story Starts

5–14 Link – Levels A and B

Writing: **Imaginative writing**
Punctuation and structure
Spelling
Handwriting and presentation
Knowledge about language

As the title above explains, these are simply the start of a story ready to be expanded by the children. This also ties in well with the new Writer's Craft part of the National Assessment for Writing. Children often find writing hard because they don't know where to start. This way they can experiment with their story writing without the pressure of 'getting started'. If a child is particularly proud of a story they have written or if you would like to keep it as evidence, simply photocopy the written-on laminate before wiping it clean.

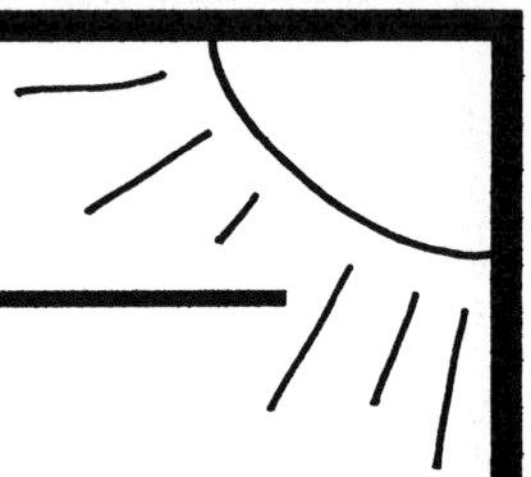

One fine, sunny day Mark went for a ride on his bike. As he was riding along he noticed a parcel lying on the path.

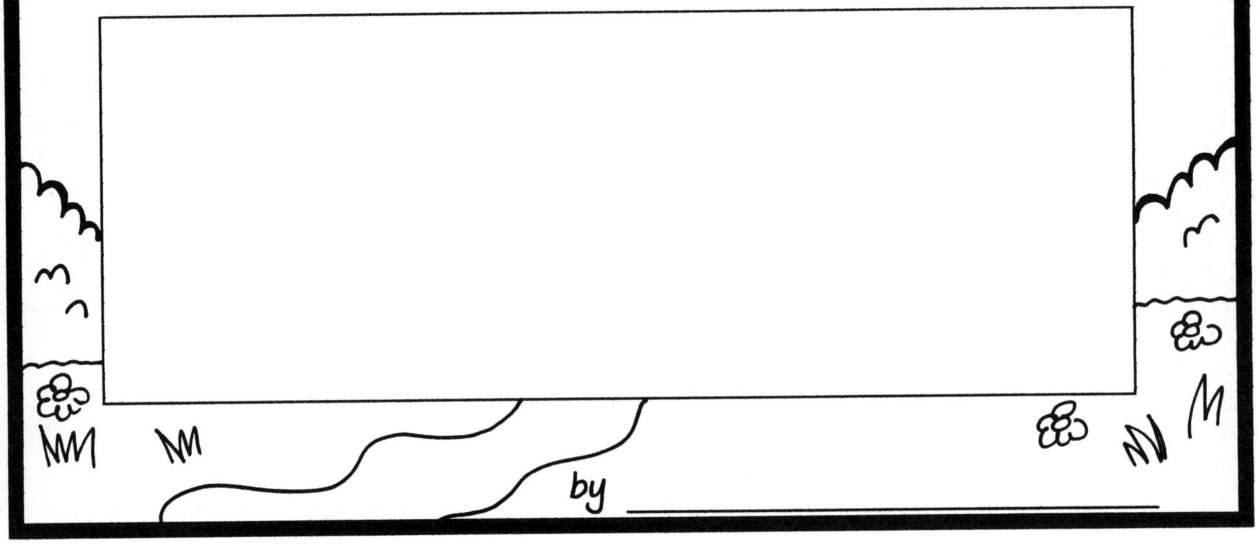

_____

_____

_____

_____

_____

_____

by _____

Once upon a time in a deep, dark forest lived an old man in a little cabin. One day he heard a knock at the door.

_____

_____

_____

_____

_____

_____

by _____

Where Am I?

5–14 Link – Levels A and B

Writing: Functional writing

Talking: Talking in groups
Conveying information, instructions and directions
Audience awareness

Listening: Listening for information, instructions and directions
Listening in groups

This activity is best done in pairs or small groups. It takes the children through their senses to describe a chosen place. Each child participating takes a laminated senses board. The location cards are cut up into strips and placed inside a bag or tub. Each child selects a location from the bag while hiding its identity from the rest of the group. They then proceed to fill out the senses board using the chosen location as a stimulus.

The children can then either read out their information or give it to their partner to read. Their aim is to guess the location. This activity is also good for exploring descriptive language for setting and location.

Teacher Tip

A timer of two or three minutes could be used to keep the children focused and to add a little bit of friendly competition.

Chapter Three: Photocopiable Resources

Where am I?

I can see

I can hear

I can smell

I can taste

I can touch

Where am I?

The park.

The seaside.

A birthday party.

The doctor's.

The dentist.

The swimming pool.

The supermarket.

The garden.

In the car.

On the bus.

On a farm.

At the fair.

At the circus.

At a football match.

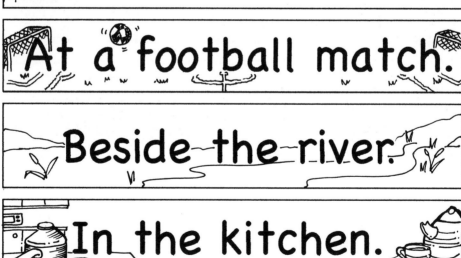

Beside the river.

In the kitchen.

In my bedroom.

In the playground.

In the classroom.

At a wedding.

In the jungle.

Re-write the Sentence

5–14 Link – Levels A and B

Writing: **Punctuation and structure**
Knowledge about language

This resource is self-explanatory and provides practice in the use of capital letters.

Re-write the sentence below, putting in the capital letters that have been missed out.

sam walked to school with her sister madeleine

_____

_____

Re-write the sentence below, putting in the capital letters that have been missed out.

lisa had a rag doll called emma

_____

_____

Re-write the sentence below, putting in the capital letters that have been missed out.

jonathan likes to go swimming on mondays

_____

_____

Re-write the sentence below, putting in the capital letters that have been missed out.

last week i went to glasgow on the train

_____

_____

Re-write the sentence below, putting in the capital letters that have been missed out.

mr steel plays football every sunday

_____

_____

Re-write the sentence below, putting in the capital letters that have been missed out.

hannah's birthday is in october

_____

_____

Re-write the sentence below, putting in the capital letters that have been missed out.

december and january are winter months

_____

_____

Re-write the sentence below, putting in the capital letters that have been missed out.

the capital city of scotland is edinburgh

_____

_____

Re-write the sentence below, putting in the capital letters that have been missed out.

nicola and alexander went shopping to glasgow

Re-write the sentence below, putting in the capital letters that have been missed out.

the taylor family went to spain in july

True, False, Can't tell

5–14 Link – Level A

Reading: Reading for information

True, False, Can't tell tasks are an excellent way of encouraging children to examine texts more closely. Some children need a lot of practice at this skill and that's why we've included a re-usable True, False, Can't tell resource sheet!

True / False / Can't tell!

Look around your classroom and answer these questions.

✓ Tick the correct box.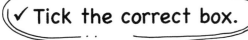

	true	false	can't tell

1. The weather is sunny.

2. The teacher has on black trousers.

3. Lunchtime is still to come.

4. My eyes are blue.

5. I have a brother.

6. Most children have apples in their lunch boxes.

7. The head teacher walked to school this morning.

8. The lollypop person is having a cup of tea.

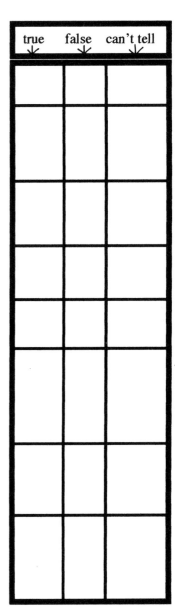

Fix the Story

5–14 Link – Levels A and B

Writing: **Punctuation and structure**
Knowledge about language
Imaginative writing

Reading: **Knowledge about language**

This resource explains itself and gives a more sustained experience of exploring the use of capital letters. The extension activity of completing the story is optional. This activity encourages the children to pay more attention to reading the text for understanding so that they can continue the story accurately. Again this provides practice in the principles of the Writer's Craft paper of the National Assessment for Writing.

Ready for blast off!

stewart put on his space helmet as he climbed into the rocket. he fastened his seat belt and waited to hear from the control tower. next the count down began. five, four, three, two, one, blast off! off went the rocket in the air. higher and higher it went up into the clouds. stewart felt excited as the rocket shook from side to side into space.

Can you find all of the missing capitals in the story? Write the next two sentences to finish the story off.

Summer sun

nicola, matthew and niamh went on their holidays in august. one sunny day they put on their shorts and t-shirts and went down to the beach to play in the sand. when they got there niamh started to fill up the buckets with sand. matthew dug out a moat while nicola collected some water from the sea. when they had finished making their castle they decorated it with shells and seaweed. suddenly, nicola noticed that the tide had started to come in.

Can you find all of the missing capitals in the story? Write the next two sentences to finish the story off.

A lonely princess

in a land far away, lived a lonely princess called anne. she lived up high in a tower in a gloomy old castle. one day, as anne looked out of her window she saw a handsome prince riding a white horse. she called on him to come and rescue her. he jumped from his horse and ran up the steps of the tower to break down the door and set her free.

Can you find all of the missing capitals in the story? Write the next two sentences to finish the story off.

Football crazy!

alan loved to play football. he played it in his garden. he played it in the park and he played it every day at school. one day alan took his football out to play. He kicked it up and down his garden and was having lots of fun. Then he tried to kick it as high up into the air as he could. as it came back down the wind caught the ball and it landed in the garden next door. he looked over the fence and saw a large, fierce dog sitting beside his ball.

Can you find all of the missing capitals in the story? Write the next two sentences to finish the story off.

Make It Better

5–14 Link – All Levels

Reading: **Knowledge about language**

Writing: **Punctuation and structure**
             Spelling
             Knowledge about language

Cut out and separate this series of simple sentences and store together in a tub or bag. The child or pair/trio choose a sentence and then re-write and embellish it with suitable adjectives and adverbs to make the sentence more interesting. For example, 'The man rode on a horse.' could be turned into 'The brave man rode gallantly on the stunning white horse'. Let their imaginations run wild. Be prepared for some funny combinations.

This resource can be used with every stage. The differentiation is in the expectation of the language generated.

The dog ran in the park.

A cat lay on the mat.

The rocket went into space.

The footballer scored a goal.

A bird flew in the sky.

The children sang a song.

The horse galloped in the field.

The dragon roared at the knight.

The fish swam in the sea.

The boy rode his bicycle.

The girl played with her doll.

The woman walked down the street.

The man drove the car.

Alphabetical Order Ideas

5–14 Link – All levels

Reading: Knowledge about language

These activities on face value are self-explanatory and would be aimed at level A/B, but there is much more that can be done with them.

✔ Enlarge the Alphabetical Order Ideas sheets to A3. For the book titles sheets, cut out the individual books and laminate them. These can then be used by the children to physically put the book titles into alphabetical order.

✔ Give the children seven or eight books from the class library to put into alphabetical order. Let them record their results on their whiteboards.

✔ As well as having titles on the side of the books we have also included authors' names. More competent children could put the books in alphabetical order according to the author's surname. This could also be done with books from their own class library.

✔ A blank topic Alphabetical Order sheet has also been included in case you wish to make your own list of topical words for the children to put into order.

✔ The blank sheet could also be given to the children to make their own list to test their partner's ability.

✔ More confident children could, after completing the Alphabetical Order task, look up the word meanings in a dictionary.

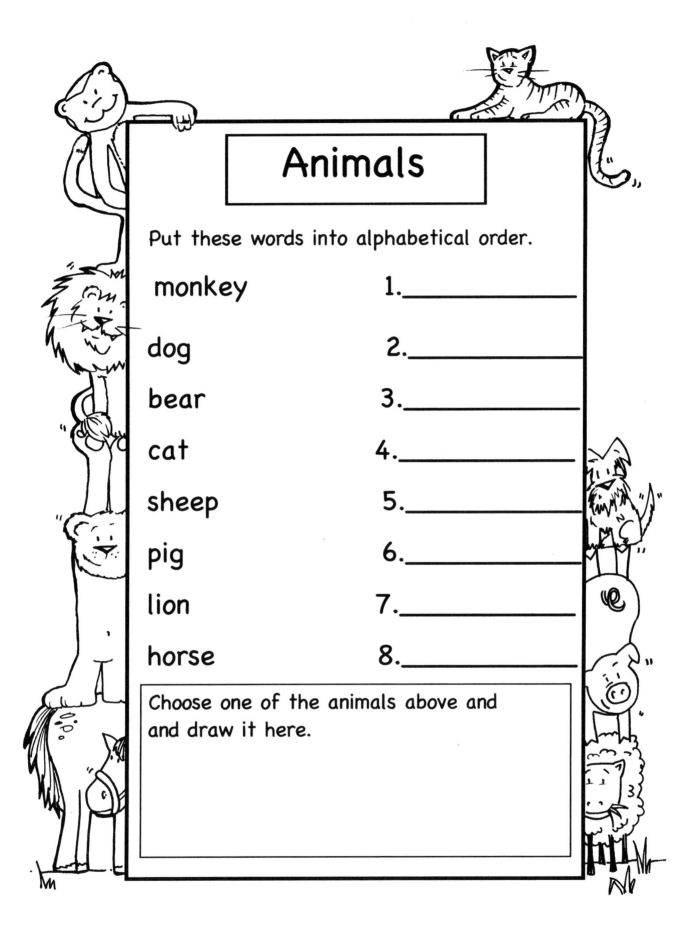

Animals

Put these words into alphabetical order.

monkey   1._____

dog   2._____

bear   3._____

cat   4._____

sheep   5._____

pig   6._____

lion   7._____

horse   8._____

Choose one of the animals above and
and draw it here.

Minibeasts

Put these words into alphabetical order.

spider   1._____

caterpillar   2._____

ladybird   3._____

ant   4._____

worm   5._____

butterfly   6._____

fly   7._____

earwig   8._____

Choose one of the minibeasts above and
and draw it here.

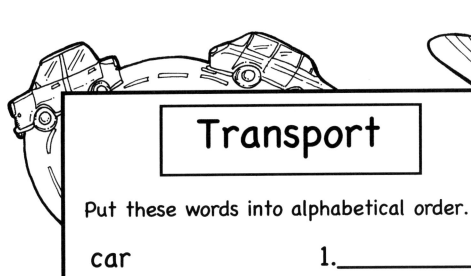

Transport

Put these words into alphabetical order.

car   1._____

van   2._____

bus   3._____

train   4._____

ship   5._____

aeroplane   6._____

walking   7._____

lorry   8._____

Choose one of the vehicles above and and draw it here.

People Who Help Us

Put these words into alphabetical order.

policeman   1._____

doctor   2._____

lollypop lady   3._____

nurse   4._____

teacher   5._____

janitor   6._____

fire fighter   7._____

cleaner   8._____

Choose one of the people above and
and draw them here.

Put these words into alphabetical order.

_____

_____

_____

_____

_____

_____

_____

_____

1._____

2._____

3._____

4._____

5._____

6._____

7._____

8._____

Choose one of the words from above and and draw it here.

Alphabetical Order

Put these book titles into alphabetical order below.

Circus
B. Topp

Bicycles
Daisy Pedal

Tents
C. Anopy

Seaside
Cliff Roks

Water
Lill Ripple

Farms
IVY MANGER

Angels
Gabriel Calling

Hats
Stetson Bowler

1. ....
2. ....
3. ....
4. ....
5. ....
6. ....
7. ....
8. ....

Alphabetical Order

Put these book titles into alphabetical order below.

Dinosaurs by T. Rex — EDWARD FURR

Teddies

Goats — Billy Kidd

Nests — A. TWIG

Plants — Holly Green

Animals — Cat Swan

Ladybirds — B. Eetle.

Insects — Ant Crawley

1. _____
2. _____
3. _____
4. _____
5. _____
6. _____
7. _____
8. _____

Alphabetical Order

Put these book titles into alphabetical order below.

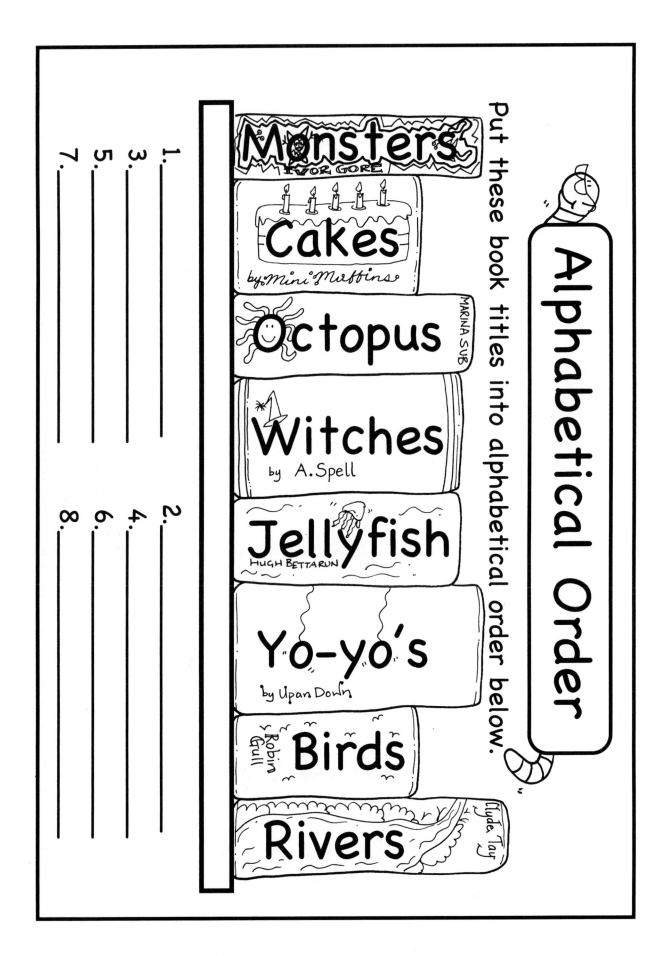

Monsters
IVOR GORE

Cakes
by Mini Muffins

Octopus
MARINA SUB

Witches
by A. Spell

Jellyfish
HUGH BETTARUN

Yo-yo's
by Upan Down

Birds
Robin Gull

Rivers
Clyde Tay

1. ....
2. ....
3. ....
4. ....
5. ....
6. ....
7. ....
8. ....

Alphabetical Order

Put these book titles into alphabetical order below.

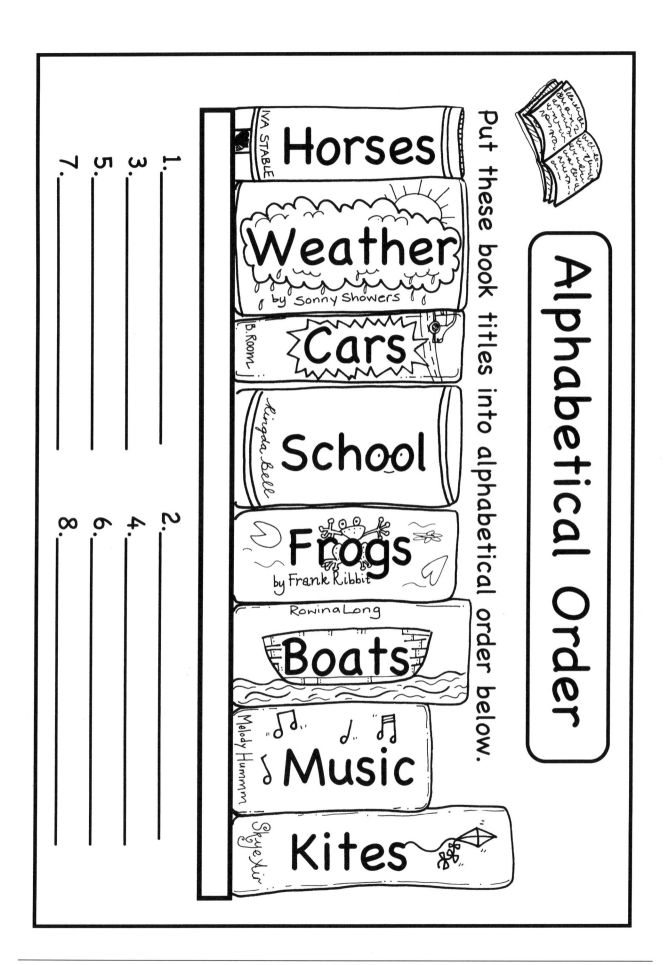

Horses — IVA STABLE

Weather — by Sonny Showers

Cars — B. Room

School — Ringda Bell

Frogs — by Frank Ribbit

Boats — Rowina Long

Music — Melody Hummm

Kites — Skye Hir

1. _____
2. _____
3. _____
4. _____
5. _____
6. _____
7. _____
8. _____

Who, What, Where, Why?

5–14 Link – Levels A and B

Reading: **Reading for enjoyment**
Awareness of genre

Writing: **Knowledge about language**
Punctuation and structure

These are, as the title suggests, a list of components to make a sentence. Each child selects one from each of the Who, What, Where and Why cards and puts them together to make a sentence. They then have to read back the sentence and, if they wish to, copy it down. It can be sensible or silly. In doing this the children are independently creating more complex and interesting sentences, as well as reinforcing the different elements of story telling and writing.

Teacher Tip

Photocopy each sheet onto a different colour of paper. This does two things:

✔ makes each different element visually distinguishable
✔ allows them to be sorted out much more easily when tidying them away.)

The little girl

The ugly witch

The brave spaceman

The funny clown

The rich king

The pretty princess

The handsome prince

The bold knight

The little old lady

The skilled footballer

The fierce dragon

was skipping along

was casting a spell

was pulling a face

was counting money

was dancing around

was riding a white horse

was holding a sword

was taking a walk

was kicking a ball

was breathing fire

was pressing buttons

Where

in the park

in a dark cave

in a rocket

in the circus ring

in the castle

in a garden

on the green hills

in the deep forest

in a busy street

on a field

in a damp dungeon

because she was happy.

because it was hallowe'en.

to make people laugh.

because it was a lovely day.

to scare people away.

because it was cold.

to win a prize.

trying to score a goal.

to get to the moon.

because it was raining.

to win the race.

Story Wordbanks

5–14 Link – A and B

Writing: **Imaginative writing**
Spelling
Knowledge about language

These are self-explanatory and allow the children to independently write stories with interesting vocabulary. Why not make the task a bit more interesting by using the large illustration on each wordbank as a template to draw around? This would make attractive paper to write their story in.

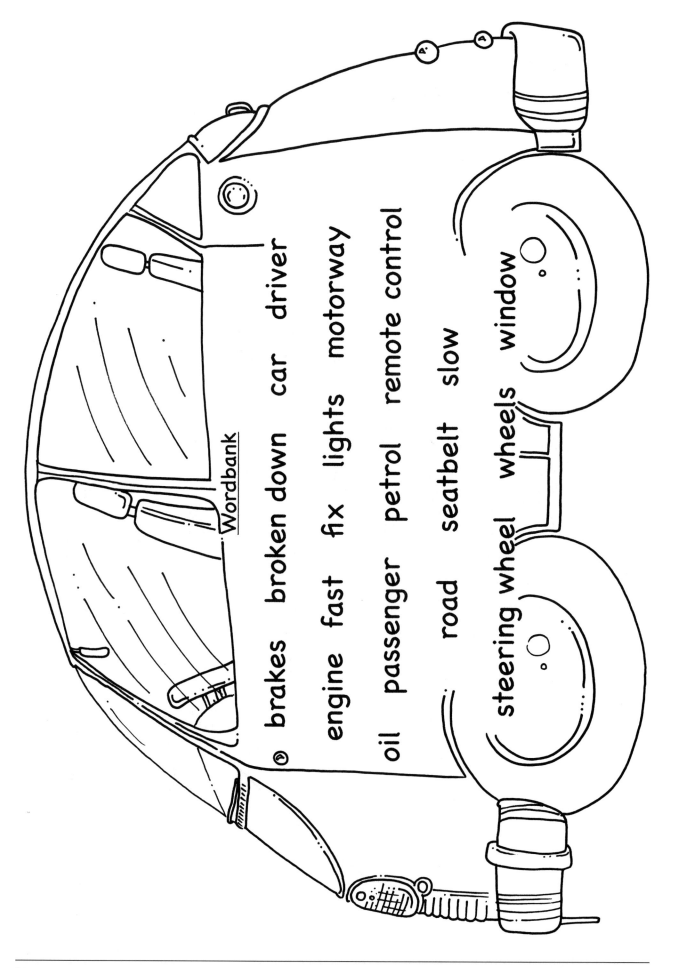

Wordbank

brakes   broken down   car   driver

engine   fast   fix   lights   motorway

oil   passenger   petrol   remote control

road   seatbelt   slow

steering wheel   wheels   window

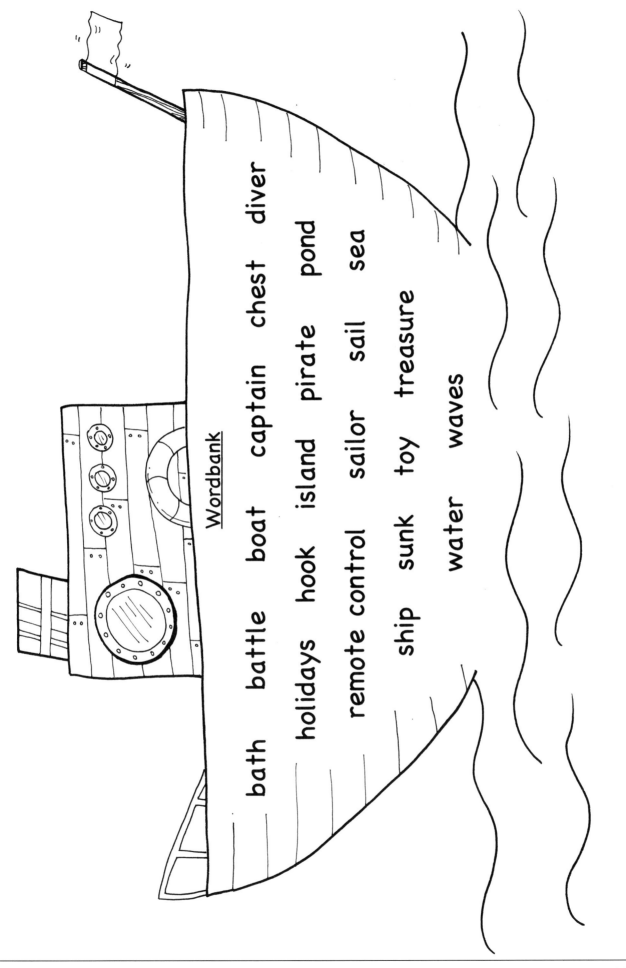

Wordbank

bath   battle   boat   captain   chest   diver

holidays   hook   island   pirate   pond

remote control   sailor   sail   sea

ship   sunk   toy   treasure

water   waves

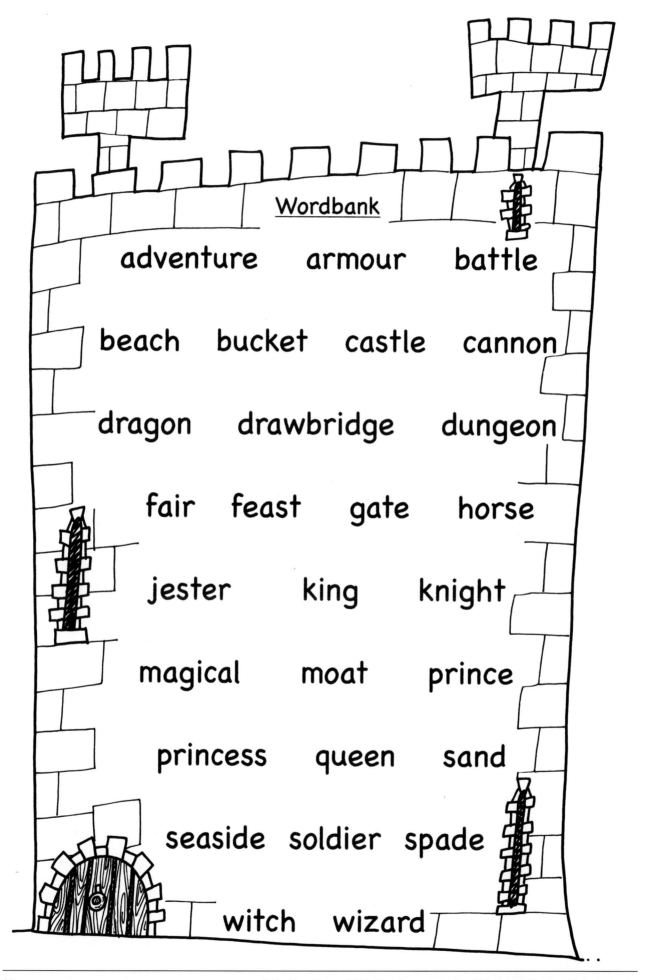

Wordbank

adventure   armour   battle

beach   bucket   castle   cannon

dragon   drawbridge   dungeon

fair   feast   gate   horse

jester   king   knight

magical   moat   prince

princess   queen   sand

seaside   soldier   spade

witch   wizard

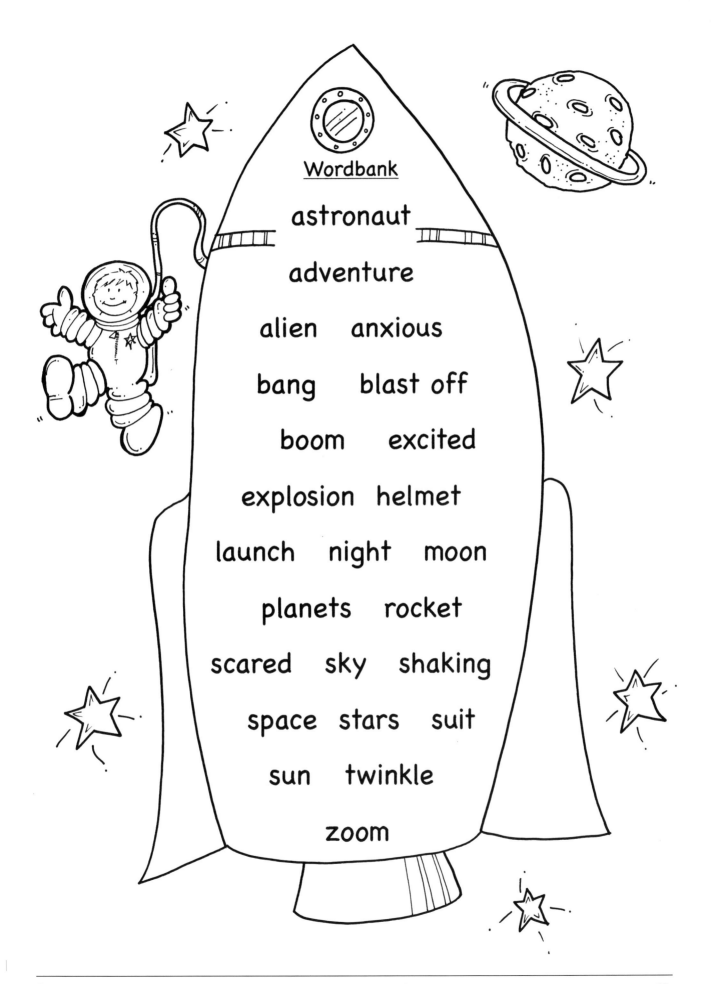

Wordbank

astronaut

adventure

alien   anxious

bang   blast off

boom   excited

explosion helmet

launch   night   moon

planets   rocket

scared   sky   shaking

space   stars   suit

sun   twinkle

zoom

Wordbank

bang   banger

bonfire   boom

crash

catherine wheel

explosion   firework

display   Guy Fawkes

fountain   glitter

light   night

rocket   sky

space   sparkler

spark   star

taper   twinkle

zoom

Sentence Bumpers

5–14 Links – All levels

Writing: **Knowledge about language**
                    Punctuation and structure
                    Spelling

Talking: **Talking in groups**

Listening: Listening in groups

These should be cut into little cards and used as a stimulus to create sentences. Each letter is used as the initial letter for each word in the sentence, for example M d l t e s could be 'My dog likes to eat sausages'. If the children are doing this in pairs or trios, let them share their responses and encourage them to discuss their word choices. Don't worry if they don't make sense at first – let them have fun with words! The differentiation in this activity comes with the expected response. They can play this over and over again choosing a new Bumper each time.

Teacher Tip

If you can, provide a timer for this activity.

A b m c a.

T l g s d.

S r p e t.

A g s l m.

M d e b c.

F d l s h.

A f b l s.

L f e s c.

T l r g d.

A s t l b.

P l c e f.

S d l r t.

T f m l s.

M b s r d.

W d y w n.

L d h f p.

C y s m l.

T r c m s.

l c s t t.

A l b d m.

W h m m g.

F d e r m.

How Many Words?

5–14 Links – Level All

Writing: Knowledge about language
Spelling

These are self-explanatory and are intended to be used as a game for pairs or small groups.

Use a timer to focus this game. To add an extra element of competition, why not assign points for each word made, for example 1 point for two- or three-letter words and more for generating words of four, five or six letters.

How many words can you make, in 1 minute, using the letters below? Can you make any 4, 5 or 6 letter words?

k i c a b m t e l

How many words can you make, in 1 minute, using the letters below? Can you make any 4, 5 or 6 letter words?

t r i s m e l p

How many words can you make, in 1 minute, using the letters below? Can you make any 4, 5 or 6 letter words?

o l t s r d e a

How many words can you make, in 1 minute, using the letters below? Can you make any 4, 5 or 6 letter words?

p e h n l a m t s

How many words can you make, in 1 minute, using the letters below? Can you make any 4, 5 or 6 letter words?

n u k f r t a c i

How many words can you make, in 1 minute, using the letters below? Can you make any 4, 5 or 6 letter words?

p b i t a d r e m

How many words can you make, in 1 minute,
using the letters below? Can you make any
4, 5 or 6 letter words?

d r e l i u t p m

How many words can you make, in 1 minute,
using the letters below? Can you make any
4, 5 or 6 letter words?

a n t r s c l m p

How many words can you make, in 1 minute,
using the letters below? Can you make any
4, 5 or 6 letter words?

j i s g o h f b p

Form Fillers

5–14 Links – Levels A and B

Writing: Functional writing

These are self-explanatory and give the children the opportunity to fill out forms that reflect personal information. For older children use real forms for them to experiment with.

Who Am I?

First Name_____

Surname_____

Middle Names_____

Date of Birth_____

My address is_____

_____

_____

_____

I live with_____

_____

I have ___brothers and ___sisters.

My school is called_____

My teacher's name is_____

My best friends are_____

_____

My favourite colour is_____

My favourite food is_____

I am good at_____

Class Helper Form

☑ Tick the job you would like to have.

Post applied for:

☐ Messenger
☐ Group Leader
☐ Line Leader
☐ Board Cleaner
☐ Cloakroom Monitor
☐ Librarian

First Name_____

Surname_____

Middle Names_____

Date of Birth_____

I would be good at this job because

Signed_____ Date_____

Recipe Card

5–14 Links – Levels A/B

Writing: Functional writing

This resource provides a template for the children to create imaginary recipes. You could, perhaps, provide a list of recipe names – though, the more independent the children are, the better.

Recipe Card

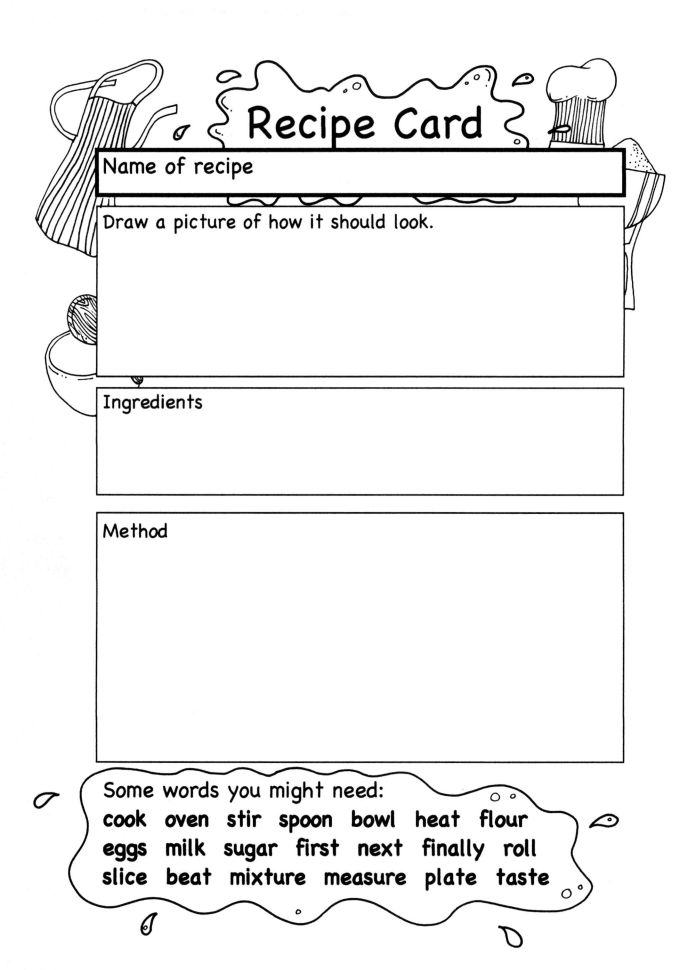

Name of recipe

Draw a picture of how it should look.

Ingredients

Method

Some words you might need:
**cook oven stir spoon bowl heat flour
eggs milk sugar first next finally roll
slice beat mixture measure plate taste**

Café Menu

5–14 Link – Levels A and B

Writing: Functional writing

This activity speaks for itself, providing a re-usable template for café fun. These could then be used during role-play situations.

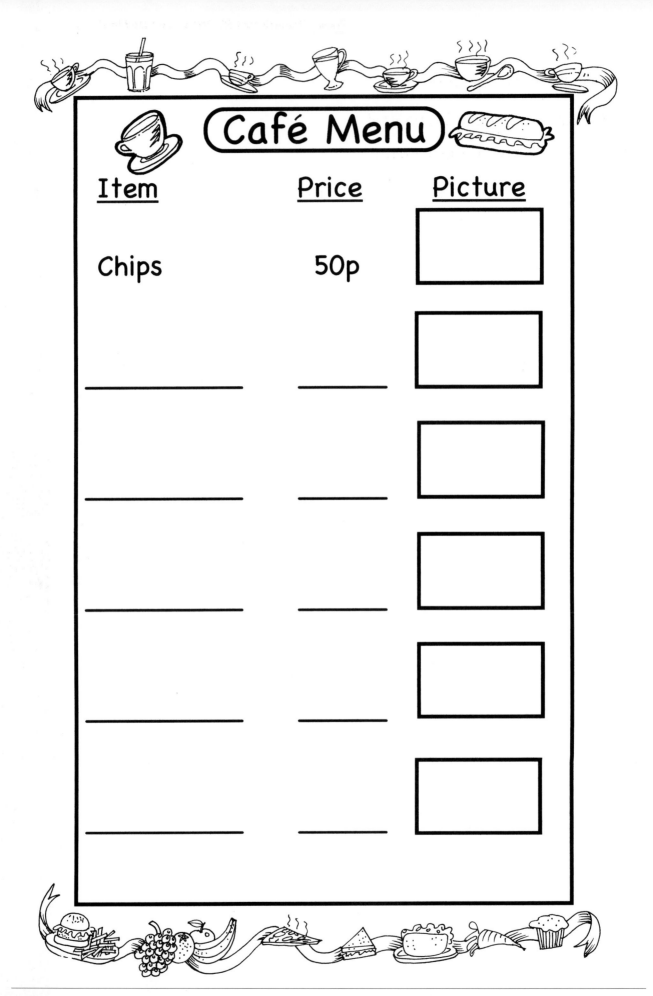

Café Menu

Item	Price	Picture
Chips	50p	
_____	_____	
_____	_____	
_____	_____	
_____	_____	
_____	_____	

Newspaper Report

5–14 Links – Levels C, D and E

Writing: **Functional writing**
Spelling
Punctuation and structure
Handwriting and presentation
Knowledge about language

This resource has a fairly obvious purpose. We suggest that you encourage the children to do this as an early finisher activity, which can be completed over a few days and could then be posted on a News Wall or placed into a News Folder and be a part of the class library (that is if they want to put it out for the rest of the class to read). Cut headlines out of real newspapers to act as a stimulus. Laminate them – they will last for ages (honestly!) Try out different themes for stories in the newspaper template, for example, stormy weather, a lottery win, an article about a local sportsman or community stories such as weddings or new exhibitions at a museum or gallery.

Reported by _____

Find the Vowel

5–14 Link – Levels B and C

Writing: Knowledge about language
Punctuation and structure

This activity explains itself. Cut the cards up to make more selection. It can be a little tricky to start with, but children love the challenge.

Find the Vowel 1

Put the missing vowels in the words below to make a sentence.

1. Th_ l_ttl_ g_rl l_st h_r d_ll.

_____

2. Th_ f_st c_r r_c_d d_wn th_ r_ _d.

_____

3. My d_g l_k_s t_ g_ f_r w_lks.

_____

4. My b_g _s bl_ck _nd r_d.

_____

Find the Vowel 2

Put the missing vowels in the words below to make a sentence.

1. Sw_tch th_ t_l_v_s_ _n _ff.

_____

2. My br_th_r l_k_s t_ w_tch c_rt_ _ ns.

_____

3. My n_w sh_ _s _r_ br_wn.

_____

4. W_ s_w m_nk_ys _t th_ z_ _.

_____

Find the Vowel 3

Put the missing vowels in the words below to make a sentence.

1. Th_ r_v_r fl_ws v_ry f_st.

_____

2. Th_ f_ _tb_ll t_ _m w_n th_ c_p.

_____

3. D_nc_ng c_n k_ _p y_ _ f_t.

_____

4. _ft_r sch_ _l w_ pl_y_d _n th_ g_rd_n.

_____

Find the Vowel 4

Put the missing vowels in the words below to make a sentence.

1. T_m_rr_w w_ _r_ g_ _ng sw_mm_ng.

_____

2. _ l_k_ t_ pl_y _n my c_mp_t_r.

_____

3. W_ p_ck_d s_m_ fl_w_rs f_r m_m.

_____

4. L_ _k b_th w_ys b_f_r_ cr_ss_ng _ r_ _ d.

_____

Dictionary Bookmarks

5–14 Link – Levels B, C and D

Reading: Knowledge about language

These bookmarks explain themselves and provide some interesting words for the children to investigate. We have provided two blank bookmarks which you can fill up with your own words.

Dictionary Bookmark
Tasks
Can you find these words in your dictionary?

Gloomy
Cheerful
Terrified
Worried
Overjoyed
Amused

✓ What do these words have in common?

✓ Put these words into alphabetical order.

✓ Write the words in your book with their definitions.

✓ If you can't find them in your dictionary write your own definition.

✓ Can you find any more words on this topic?

Dictionary Bookmark
Tasks
Can you find these words in your dictionary?

Joint
Vein
Artery
Tissue
Organ
Cartilage

✓ What do these words have in common?

✓ Put these words into alphabetical order.

✓ Write the words in your book with their definitions.

✓ If you can't find them in your dictionary write your own definition.

✓ Can you find any more words on this topic?

Dictionary Bookmark Tasks

Can you find these words in your dictionary?

Thunder
Storm
Calm
Sleet
Shower
Fair

- ✓ What do these words have in common?

- ✓ Put these words into alphabetical order.

- ✓ Write the words in your book with their definitions.

- ✓ If you can't find them in your dictionary write your own definition.

- ✓ Can you find any more words on this topic?

Dictionary Bookmark Tasks

Can you find these words in your dictionary?

_____
_____
_____
_____
_____
_____
_____
_____
_____

- ✓ What do these words have in common?

- ✓ Put these words into alphabetical order.

- ✓ Write the words in your book with their definitions.

- ✓ If you can't find them in your dictionary write your own definition.

- ✓ Can you find any more words on this topic?

Dictionary Bookmark Tasks

Can you find these words in your dictionary?

Haunt
Residence
Habitat
Dwelling
Abode
Domicile
Domain

✓ What do these words have in common?

✓ Put these words into alphabetical order.

✓ Write the words in your book with their definitions.

✓ If you can't find them in your dictionary write your own definition.

✓ Can you find any more words on this topic?

Dictionary Bookmark Tasks

Can you find these words in your dictionary?

- - - - - - - - - - - - - - - -
- - - - - - - - - - - - - - - -
- - - - - - - - - - - - - - - -
- - - - - - - - - - - - - - - -
- - - - - - - - - - - - - - - -
- - - - - - - - - - - - - - - -
- - - - - - - - - - - - - - - -
- - - - - - - - - - - - - - - -
- - - - - - - - - - - - - - - -

✓ What do these words have in common?

✓ Put these words into alphabetical order.

✓ Write the words in your book with their definitions.

✓ If you can't find them in your dictionary write your own definition.

✓ Can you find any more words on this topic?

Dictionary Bookmark Tasks

Can you find these words in your dictionary?

Tornado
Hurricane
Drizzle
Blizzard
Hazy
Gale
Humid
Zephyr
Isobar

✓ What do these words have in common?

✓ Put these words into alphabetical order.

✓ Write the words in your book with their definitions.

✓ If you can't find them in your dictionary write your own definition.

✓ Can you find any more words on this topic?

Dictionary Bookmark Tasks

Can you find these words in your dictionary?

Petrified
Elated
Contented
Miserable
Confused
Flabbergasted
Astounded
Reserved
Timid

✓ What do these words have in common?

✓ Put these words into alphabetical order.

✓ Write the words in your book with their definitions.

✓ If you can't find them in your dictionary write your own definition.

✓ Can you find any more words on this topic?

Novel Titles

5–14 Links – Levels C, D and E

Writing: **Imaginative writing**
Punctuation and structure
Spelling
Knowledge about language

Refer to chapter 2 page 11 for more detailed information on how to use this resource.

The Lonely Road

THE BROKEN MIRROR

The Curse of the Emerald Ring

A Big Win

One Goal to Glory

Bring on the Bullies

MISSING

The Secret Letter

You Can't Run Forever

Behind the Door in the Hall

Friends Forever

A Broken Promise

Anything But Said!

5–14 Link – Levels C and D

Reading: Knowledge about language

Writing: Punctuation and structure

This resource explains itself. It focuses on the punctuation and structure of direct speech in pupils' writing.

Anything but <u>Said</u>! 1

Punctuate these sentences putting speech marks, commas and full stops in the correct places.

1. It's so beautiful gushed Tina holding the gift in her hand I can't believe you remembered my birthday

_____

_____

_____

2. I don't think I can do it sighed Martin reluctantly I haven't got any spare time today

_____

_____

_____

3. I have something to tell you whispered Maryann cautiously but you can't tell anyone about it

_____

_____

_____

Anything but Said! 2

Punctuate these sentences putting speech marks, commas and full stops in the correct places.

1. If you cared at all sneered Claire angrily you would know that John was sick and couldn't come to the party

_____

_____

_____

2. It will be alright reassured Lynn you will get it finished on time

_____

_____

_____

3. I don't like that one muttered Alistair to himself I wanted the other prize

_____

_____

_____

Anything but Said! 3

Punctuate these sentences putting speech marks, commas and full stops in the correct places.

1. I don't see why groaned Hardip I have to be the one who has to tidy up your mess

_____

_____

_____

2. Where are you going screamed Leah to Jasmine we are depending on you to go too

_____

_____

_____

3. There is just one thing I would like to know quizzed Ayesha menacingly why did you leave the golden arrow behind

_____

_____

_____

Boring to Brilliant

5–14 Links – Levels C and D

Reading: Knowledge about language

This activity is self-explanatory. It encourages the use of the thesaurus in their pupils' own writing.

Boring to Brilliant!

Rewrite the sentences below changing the underlined words by using a thesaurus.

1. In the <u>dark</u> woods stood a <u>little</u> <u>old</u> cottage.

_____

_____

2. The <u>angry</u> man shouted at the <u>bad</u> dog.

_____

_____

3. A <u>large</u> green plant stood on the <u>shiny</u> wooden floor.

_____

_____

4. The house felt <u>cold</u> and had a <u>damp</u> smell.

_____

_____

Boring to Brilliant!

Rewrite the sentences below changing the underlined words by using a thesaurus.

1. Catrina <u>looked</u> at the <u>little</u> girl and smiled.

_____

_____

2. A <u>bright</u> star <u>shone</u> in the <u>dark</u> sky.

_____

_____

3. The <u>sad</u> film made Mark feel <u>upset</u>.

_____

_____

4. The <u>happy</u> cat purred when it felt <u>happy</u>.

_____

_____

Boring to Brilliant!

Rewrite the sentences below changing the underlined words by using a thesaurus.

1. John heard a loud noise coming from the <u>empty</u> cellar.

_____

_____

2. The <u>small</u> mouse ran <u>quickly</u> across the floor into a <u>dark</u> corner.

_____

_____

3. The <u>fast</u> rabbit <u>jumps</u> over the <u>low</u> fence.

_____

_____

4. I felt <u>happy</u> when we won the <u>lovely</u> prize.

_____

_____

Punctuate!

5–14 Links – Levels C and D

Reading: **Awareness of genre**
Knowledge about language

Writing: **Punctuation and structure**
Knowledge about language

This resource explains itself. This can be quite a difficult activity, but it focuses well on defining sentence structure. The final activity of continuing the story fits in well with the Writer's Craft section of the National Assesment for Writing.

Punctuate! 1

Punctuate the paragraph below.

Amy picked up her school bag and left for school with the same heavy heart as yesterday itll be alright today comforted her mum she probably wont even look at you mum smiled but Amy could tell that beneath the smile mum was worried Shannon had been picking on Amy since primary four and recently things had become worse and it wasnt just name calling Shannon had started taking things from Amy and was now threatening to hurt her

Write the next few sentences of the story.

Punctuate! 2

Punctuate the paragraph below.

come on boy shouted Steven to his dog come on its time to go home Sam was a large black Labrador who belonged to the whole family but it was Steven who paid him the most attention and took him out for his daily walk to the park come on boy Steven yelled again but Sam did not move he was sniffing the ground and staring at something in the bushes with a sigh Steven walked over to investigate little did he know that his life was about to change

Write the next few sentences of the story.

Punctuate! 3

Punctuate the paragraph below.

It was a beautiful crisp morning when Jonathan and William decided to go down to the local park to kick around their football on the way they stopped off at the corner shop to buy a snack and something to drink Jonathan put his hand into his pocket to get some money its gone gasped Jonathan my money is gone did you leave it at home said William no I definitely had it with me replied Jonathan searching both of his pockets

Write the next few sentences of the story.

Punctuate! 4

Punctuate the paragraph below.

Helen opened her eyes and looked out into the gloom of her darkened room what had been the noise that had woken her up from her sleep she felt around for her dressing gown and pulled it on bang she heard it again hello her voice wavered is there anybody there she hesitated before moving from her bed towards the door hello slowly she placed her hand upon the door handle

Write the next few sentences of the story.

Award

5–14 Links – All levels

Writing: Functional writing

This is here for the children to award their peers with a certificate for any reason. If it is laminated, the certificate can remain on their desk for the day before being wiped and placed back into the writing box.

Award

This award for _____

Goes to _____

From _____

Well Done!

Play Dough Recipes

No-Cook Play Dough

- 1 cup salt
- 1 cup flour
- 1 tablespoon oil
- Food colouring
- Water

Mix dry ingredients; add oil.
Add food colouring to water
Slowly add water until desired
consistency is ready.

Cooked Play Dough

- 1 cup flour
- 1/2 cup salt
- 2 teaspoons cream of tartar
- 1 cup water
- 1 tablespoon oil
- Food colouring

Combine flour, salt, and cream
of tartar in a saucepan. Mix
liquids and gradually stir them
into dry ingredients. When
mixture is smooth, cook over
medium heat, stirring
constantly until a ball forms.
Remove from heat and knead
until smooth. This is a very
pliable and long-lasting play
dough, with a more elastic
consistency than uncooked
play dough.